Ireland's Wildlife

FOR RITA
MY FRIEND, MY INSPIRATION
AND THE LOVE OF MY LIFE.

Ireland's Wildlife

A Photographic Essay
By Mike Brown

With Foreword
By Dick Warner

Published in 2002
by Mike Brown Photography,
Knockaveale, Bandon, Co Cork, Ireland.

Design by Bart Van Put, Antwerp, Belgium.

Printed in Belgium by Daneels Graphic Group.

All photographs and captions © Mike Brown.
Foreword © Dick Warner.
All other text © Mike Brown.

Cataloguing in publication. A CIP catalogue record
for this book is available from the British Library.

ISBN 0-9542863-0-8

Above. An Arctic tern feeds its chick while on the
wing.

Half title page. A Kingfisher rests on a riverbank
branch.

Page 2. A wild poppy blooms in a barley field.

Title page. Fungi colonises a rotting tree trunk.

Prints of the photographs in this book
may be purchased by contacting

Mike Brown Photography
on +353 86 8295039 or at
www.mikebrownphotography.com.

Contents

Acknowledgements

For much of the time, wildlife photography can be an extremely solitary existence. I often spend hours on end cooped up in a cramped hide in which I can barely stretch my legs. This can be hard on the patience as well as the joints. If the creature that I'm chasing does come to the right spot however and I'm quick enough to make the picture I want, then the reward always outweighs the hardship. While these lonely excursions can be the norm within my work, they are often only possible because of work done or information given to me by another wildlife lover.

This book would not have been possible without the enormous amount of help I received from many people. Some simply rang to say they had seen something of interest. Others physically helped me setting up positions from which to do the photography or shared their wonderful and detailed knowledge about a specific subject. Many of these people only came in contact with me when I approached them about this project but are now firm friends. It is simply not possible to repay the debt to some of those who assisted me during the last three years as I traversed the country in search of new subjects and new pictures, as their help went far beyond what I could expect. All I can do is offer my sincere and heartfelt thanks and hope that they too can enjoy the end result. To those listed here my gratitude is eternal and to any I have forgotten along the way, my sincere apologies.

My mother Annabel for all her wonderful support. My grandfather Dennis, for instilling in me a love of everything wild. Jeremy and Annette for all their help and info. To the rest of my family in Courtmacsherry for their help in any way. Pete and Fran Wolstenholme for their great friendship over many years and much more. Andy for his encouragement and for editing some of the text for this book. Steve and Caroline Marquart in Kilbrittain, for their incredible support, encouragement and friendship. Mike and June Fox for their help and info over the years. Mike O'Sullivan [Clonakilty] for bird advice. Pat and David Lamb and of course mum Poojie.

Phil Davis, Paul Moore, and Tony Nagle of the Cork branch of Bird Watch Ireland for great advice and letting me showcase my work to their members. Mike O'Sullivan [Knocknagree], for his help and his immense enthusiasm for nature and my photography. At Bird Watch Ireland in Dublin, Stephen Newton for making many things possible and Oran O'Sullivan and Declan Murphy for their help.

Bill and Deirdre Johnson and the staff at Colour Foto in Cork for their true understanding, with a special thanks to Billy for processing all my slides and pushing and pulling my film when necessary. Ali Purden at the Helme for her assistance and hard work. Billy Skuse at TSB Bandon for having faith. Denis Mac and his staff at Denis MacSweeney photo shop for their help over the years. Kieran and his staff at O'Leary's Camera World ditto. Steve Baker at Leeds Photographic in London for his great help with equipment. Damien Enright for his enthusiasm and some excellent publicity. Duchas Wildlife Rangers Pat Smiddy, Michael O'Sullivan and Tim O'Donoghue. Oscar Merne, Bernard Moloney, Ruth O'Sullivan and Noreen Kerins at Duchas for their assistance. Juanita, Declan, Vinny, Helen, Colm and the team at Wild Ireland, for showcasing my work and lots more. Bryan and Sara Deegan for loads of help and encouragement.

Martin and Lynda Smyth in Wexford for a comfortable place to stay and lots of info. Marian and Kemp Cooper in Bandon for letting me camp in their garden. Tom Cleary in Nenagh for help with his feathered friends. Tom and Sheila O'Hanlon in Cork for giving me the run of their house and garden. Con Kelleher for his advice. Arthur and Ruth Cole for thinking of me when they had something of interest. Oliver O'Cadhla for his help with seals. A special thanks to Des Bateman, who sadly passed away without seeing the fruits of my work with his friends in the garden. To fellow photographers Eddie Dunne and Billy Clarke for some fun up north. A special thanks to Kevin Collins, for his immense knowledge, his hard work and for introducing me to some of our special inhabitants and to Sinead and Cliona for their hospitality.

To my parents in law Leon and Josée without whom this project would never have been started and for their encouragement. To Bart for putting this project together so beautifully.

Finally to my wife Rita and the kids Matthew, Rosie, Brad and Sarah who had to put up with me being away a lot during this project. Without all your love and support none of this would have happened.

Patrons

The publication of this book would not have been possible without the generous support of those shown on this page. To each of them my eternal thanks.

Schering-Plough (Brinny) Company

Niall O'Driscoll • Gearóid O'Driscoll • Dan Murphy

82 North Main St., Bandon, Co. Cork

Georgia-Pacific Ireland

An Chomhairle Oidhreachta   The Heritage Council

This publication has received support from the Heritage Council under the 2002 Publications Grant Scheme.

Foreword

Islands are usually not well off when it comes to wildlife. They have fewer species of plants and animals than places that are part of a continental land mass. Ireland is an island off an island, and it has been that way for at least ten thousand years. Because of this our list of native species is quite short. If we take mammals as an example, Ireland has only half the number of carnivore species that Britain has and only a quarter of the rodent species.

Human beings have also managed to exterminate some of this impoverished heritage of wildlife. Corn Buntings became extinct in Ireland at the end of the twentieth century as a result of changing agricultural practice. The Rannoch Rush became extinct in the 1950s as a result of bog drainage and exploitation. Wolves were finally exterminated in the eighteenth century because they preyed on livestock and the Wild Boar became extinct some time in the early Middle Ages because of hunting pressure and the destruction of woodlands.

But it's not all bad news — far from it.

The isolation of islands can lead to the evolution of new species. This is what Charles Darwin observed in the Galapagos Islands and it led him to develop the Theory of Evolution. Ireland has only been isolated for ten to twelve thousand years and this is not long enough for a wide range of uniquely Irish endemic species to develop. But we do have some. Most of them are freshwater fish, like the Killarney Shad and the Pollan. There is also one endemic tree, the Irish Whitebeam, and a number of very interesting Irish sub-species. Four of our bird species are recognised as separate sub-species — the Irish Dipper, the Irish Coal Tit, the Irish Jay and the Irish Red Grouse. The Irish Hare is possibly our most interesting sub-species. It is a race of the European Mountain Hare and the main difference is that Ireland is the only place in the world where this species does not turn white in winter an adaptation to our mild climate and lack of snow.

And, though human beings have been responsible for the extermination of some of our heritage of wildlife, the list of introductions far out-numbers the extinctions. Trees are a good example of this. Something like three hundred species of tree grow in Ireland and only about twenty-eight are native. More than half of our freshwater fish species were introduced by humans and so were such familiar countryside inhabitants as Pheasants, Rabbits, Hedgehogs and Grey Squirrels.

Our wildlife is also enriched by an unusual amount of seasonal visitors from abroad. Most of these migrants are birds, though we do get some spectacular migrant butterflies and moths in late summer — species like the Red Admiral, the Painted Lady, the Clouded Yellow and the Hummingbird Hawk Moth.

What makes Ireland so attractive to migrant birds is a virtually unique combination of high latitude and mild climate. The high latitude ensures that in summer the days are long. Breeding birds need a long day in order to collect enough food for themselves and their brood. So in summer we attract birds from the south where the days are shorter.

In winter Ireland is the most northerly place in Europe or North America where ice and snow are uncommon and short-lived. So birds from as far away as western Greenland or Siberia flock in to feed. Most of them are either water birds and wetland birds escaping ice or else grazing birds escaping snow. But we do get some smaller winter migrants like Fieldfares and Bramblings and some birds of prey, like the Short Eared Owl. There are also resident Irish birds, such as Starlings and Woodcock, whose numbers are increased enormously in winter by refugees from colder places.

One other thing that contributes to the richness of Irish wildlife is the fact that our landscape is a relatively friendly place for wild plants and animals. It is a completely man-made landscape. We have no wilderness. Even the blanket bog on our mountains or the limestone pavement in the Burren is there because human beings destroyed the forests. But although it is artificial it is fairly unspoiled compared to most of the rest of western Europe.

Most of Ireland escaped the Industrial Revolution of the mid-nineteenth century and much of it escaped the Agricultural Revolution of the mid-Twentieth century. We also have a relatively low population density. As a result Ireland and western Scotland are the only places left that have healthy populations of the European Otter — a species that a couple of centuries ago had a range from here eastwards to Japan and southwards to North Africa.

Because intensive tillage farming and the use of agri-chemicals are uncommon in Ireland and declining we have more winged insects than most European countries where they have been killed by pesticides.

This also means we have internationally important populations of some bat species that feed exclusively on winged insects. But the decline in tillage, in particular in traditional cereal growing, has been unfortunate for a small group of wild species that depended on this sort of activity. The extinction of the Corn Bunting has already been mentioned. The Grey Partridge is on the verge of extinction and so is the wild Corn Flower.

There is also a lot of variety in the landscape of this small island. We have an enormously long coastline — over four thousand kilometres, which is more than the coastline of France. Our coastal wildlife is very rich and at certain times of the year we are visited by huge numbers of oceanic birds that have to breed on the land. Even more exciting are the marine mammals that visit us — in particular the whales and dolphins. Interest in these has grown massively in recent years and now we realise that Ireland is the best country in Europe for whale watching.

Irish coastal waters are being grossly over-fished and they have some pollution problems, notably from salmon farming. This has implications for the delicate marine food chains and the next generation may not be able to enjoy the wealth of coastal wildlife that is still with us today. We have more than our fair share of fresh water too and many of our rarest plants, animals and birds are associated with bogs, callows, lakes and rivers. The worrying thing is that we are now the only country in western Europe where both ground water and surface water are becoming more polluted every year. The largest single cause of this pollution is livestock farming and if we fail to tackle the problems it poses we risk losing many of the finest jewels in the wildlife crown.

We still have some interesting scraps of woodland left and, whilst we don't have high mountains, we have considerable areas of upland that support their own special fauna and flora. In fact one of the things that excites foreign botanists when they come to Ireland is that you can find plant species here growing quite close to one another which would normally be separated by thousands of metres of altitude or many degrees of latitude. On one small island we have arctic, alpine, temperate and Mediterranean wild plants.

So we are very lucky. We have a much more varied and fascinating flora and fauna than we should have. It is not just there to be studied, it is also to be enjoyed. That is what this book is about. It is not a text book and has no pretensions to being either comprehensive or even particularly scientific. It is a celebration. A celebration in Mike's wonderful photographs of some facets of the natural wonder that surrounds us on this island.

My hope is that these photographs will increase your awareness of our natural heritage and increase your love of it. This is vitally important if conservation is to succeed. People only conserve the things that they love.

Dick Warner

Introduction

During my childhood, my grandfather introduced me to the wonders of the natural world. Although a leader in the field of industrial chemistry during his working life, he had enjoyed a love of nature since he was young and he passed as much of this on to his family as he could.

When pointing out something of interest, he always showed an equal passion, whether it was a real star of the wildlife world like a peregrine falcon or a simple fungi growing from the side of a fallen tree. His other great hobby, which could have easily been his profession, was

painting in watercolours. He would spend many hours sitting quietly in the open landscape, with his pad on his knee as he first made preliminary sketches and then created a beautiful painting. His patience and his love for the beauty of wild places and wild creatures were inspiring for a youngster. I now know that most of my appreciation of our wonderful wildlife comes from early days in his company.

In Ireland we are lucky to have many places where we can see wildlife quite easily. However, we often look without seeing the true beauty of our subject. When I started this project I wanted to create a set of images that show some of our wildlife in all its glory. I am not a scientist and this is not a scientific book. Neither is it supposed to be a compendium of all the wild creatures that exist in Ireland. Some readers may comment that a certain species has been excluded from these pages but this was never the point of this book. In my mind, all our wildlife is of equal stature. Some species may be close to extinction, some may be almost too numerous but all have an individual beauty if we care to look.

The following pages contain a personal selection of images, edited from many more that I made during this project. It represents just a small fraction of the wild beauty we share our island with. With this great diversity of wildlife in our land, we should count ourselves as truly fortunate.

Much of my work is done alone but I get great enjoyment from sharing my images and stories of my wildlife encounters with others. I hope that as you move through the pages of this book, you can feel the same sense of wonder that I feel, whenever I look through the viewfinder of my camera.

Mike Brown

The Photographs

As evening falls, gentle waves brush over the rocks along a stretch of the West Cork coastline. The rise and fall of the tide is a true constant in an ever-changing country.

Around our Coastline

I didn't feel I could publish a book of photographs of Ireland's wildlife without including "Fungi" the Dingle dolphin.

Fungi is a Bottle-nosed Dolphin and is probably Ireland's most famous wild creature. Seen by thousands of people each year as they take boat trips from Dingle, he rarely disappoints viewers and usually comes alongside the boats. To see a dolphin swimming in close up like this is a great pleasure and shows the tremendous power they have as they cut through the water.

⇧ The eggs of the Little tern are hard to distinguish from the shingle, as an adult settles to incubate at Kilcoole, Co Wicklow. The male and female share incubation duties, swapping regularly so that each has a chance to feed. Wardens are in constant attendance during the breeding season to give these delicate birds every chance of successfully raising young. To keep the eggs and chicks safe, an electric fence is erected around the perimeter of the colony, to keep foxes and stray dogs away.

A Common tern calls at its breeding colony on Rockabill ⇨ lighthouse station. With roseate and arctic terns as well as various other seabirds breeding here, Rockabill is a maelstrom of noise and action. It gives a feeling of exhilaration to a wildlife lover like myself to see this close up. The noise at times can be deafening and sturdy headgear is advisable in a place like this, as if you stray too close to the nesting areas the birds show their annoyance by flying at you, often pecking the top of your head with their sharp bills.

Usually seen on beaches and mud flats the Oystercatcher often ventures onto fields and pastures to feed. Getting close to this bird reveals a deep red eye, which contrasts beautifully with its black and white plumage.

A juvenile Grey heron pulls a lugworm from a small tidal pool in Cork harbour. I was working from a hide and the bird was unaware of my presence. At one stage it came so close that my telephoto lens was unable to focus on it. ⇨

Water droplets slide down the back of a Ringed plover as it sits on its eggs in the rain. I had found this one on a beach close to home a few days before and had earmarked it for a picture.

When I saw the rain pouring down on this particular morning, I couldn't resist going down and making this image of a bird loyal to its cause come rain or shine.

Grey seal pups look cute with their fluffy white fur but can inflict a nasty bite if you were to get too close. The pups remain on a nursery beach often in large numbers and the adult females come in periodically to suckle them.

I was photographing Gannets on their nests and in the air above the colony when I noticed this one lunging forward periodically as if protecting its space. Seeing this as an opportunity for a different type of image, I got on my hands and knees and with a wide-angle lens got as close as I thought was safe!

Razorbills look very elegant in their striking black and white plumage. This one, which is resting between fishing trips, contrasts beautifully with the deep blue of the sea in the background.

A seabird colony is a noisy and smelly place with birds clustered shoulder to shoulder on the rocks and cliff faces.

This Guillemot was standing amongst a group of many birds looking a little bemused with such a large catch in its bill and didn't seem to know what to do with it.

A young Common seal rests on a rock in the harbour near Glengarriff, Co. Cork. One of the best ways to see these seals is to take a ferry to nearby Garnish island. ⇨

If there were a prize for hairstyles in the bird world, the Red-breasted Merganser would win it every time. This is the female of the species, which is far less colourful than the male but which sports the same spiky tufts on its head.

The Little Egret, seen here catching a crab, has become a common sight in Ireland again recently. This beautiful bird is now breeding here successfully after many years of absence.

The deep purple blooms of Heather are common on many hills and moors in Ireland. Here it adds a wonderful splash of colour to this coastal landscape on a bright morning in early August.

(previous spread) A pair of Common Dolphins surge through the water as they bow-ride a fishing boat. These beautiful creatures are found in many places around Ireland and often congregate in large groups. The power and agility they exhibit as they swim alongside boats is truly awesome and they seem to do it with minimal effort. Dolphins always appear to have a special effect on man and our relationship with them is one which is seems to be filled with a sense of well-being.

A Fulmar broods its single egg on a cliff face. Care must be taken when approaching these birds, as their method of defence is to vomit their fishy stomach contents at those who stray too close.

This Otter had been seen feeding near a boatyard on an estuary quite regularly. It was wintertime, which is often a good time to see otters on the coast. After fishing offshore for a while it climbed onto a pontoon and sat in a tyre to rest. The weather was dark and gloomy, making photography difficult but for a few minutes the sky brightened and I took this second picture as it made its way back to the water. ✎ ⇧

The rocks behind this Shag were almost completely covered with bird droppings making them almost pure white.

This contrasted beautifully with the dark plumage of the bird. Its emerald green eye and the yellow in its bill add some colour to an otherwise monochrome image.

An Arctic tern arrives to feed its waiting chick on a beach in County Wexford. The birds nest on small islands on the lake at Lady's Island nearby. When the chicks are first able to fly the adults encourage them down to the beach so that their trips with food are shortened considerably. The action is fast and furious when an adult arrives, as many of the chicks call expectantly. The adults recognise their own chicks by their specific call and usually deliver the food without bothering to touch down. To get a nice image requires quick reactions as the chicks run down the beach to meet the adults and it is all over in a matter of seconds. ⇨

If you sit quietly by the seashore, Dunlins will often come quite close as they forage for food on the tide-line. This bird was photographed in late July and has the dark under parts of its summer plumage.

The strong shape and spectacular colours of the Puffin's bill make it instantly recognisable. These pretty birds can be seen on many seabird colonies around the coast. I chose to shoot an extreme close-up of this one, which was fresh from a fishing trip, to show these wonderful features fully. ⇨

Woodlands, Parks and Gardens

Bluebells covering a woodland floor in springtime is one of the great colour spectacles in Irish nature. Here they combine with Ramsons [a wild garlic], and the beautiful greens of a woodland spring, to create a superb mix of colour and contrast.

The male Pheasant is one of the most brightly coloured birds in the land.
Introduced originally for game shooting, it is now common all over the
country. This one was a regular visitor to a garden and it would stand
under bird feeders that were placed in a tree, in the hope that some nuts
and seeds would fall its way.

Pine Martens are very secretive and not often seen. Food was put out at this wall in a small wood in the Burren in Co. Clare and this animal often came for a free feed after dark. After being offered a wide range of foods it was discovered that it was particularly partial to whipped cream!!

The Tortoiseshell is one of our most common butterflies but its bright colours make it very attractive to the eye. When I photograph butterflies I try to find specimens which are as near to perfect as possible, as many get damaged and weather beaten quite quickly. I photographed this one in my own garden as it rested on a plant.

Oyster mushrooms are hard to miss on a woodland floor due to their large size. While this makes them look very robust, a view of their underside reveals a more delicate image. ⇦⇨

The Song thrush is always busy in spring and sometimes raises three broods of young in a season. Because of this it needs to be an expert at collecting worms, grubs and snails to feed its hungry hatchlings.

The Wood Anemone is one of our most delicate woodland plants. Flowering in early spring it adds some of the first colour to the woodland floor each year. They are usually clustered together in groups but I spotted this one that seemed isolated and felt it showed the beautiful quality of this pretty plant. ⇨

With its black cap, white cheeks and yellow belly the Great tit is a striking bird. Common in gardens, woodlands and hedgerows, it is a regular visitor to the bird table during the winter months. This one was photographed at my own bird table where I set up perches for the birds to land on as they come and go.

The Grey Squirrel is native to north America but has been resident in Britain for many years. Now established in Ireland also it is bigger than the red squirrel and seems to tolerate humans more easily.

I photographed this squirrel as it stripped bark from a tree in the National Botanic gardens in Glasnevin, Dublin where they cohabit with red squirrels.

Coal tits, which are one of our smallest tit species, are regulars at a winter bird table. This one would always stop on this post that I had set up at the side of the garden, before going to the hanging feeders.

50

This Poplar Hawk Moth was found resting on a pile of discarded wood during the day. After making the first photo I wanted to show a more interesting view. By carefully lifting the piece of wood into a different position and using some flash lighting I was able to show the strange front view of this moth. After the work was done it was returned to its resting place.

With a shaded forest in the background, Rosebay willow herb shines brightly in the light of the setting sun. Also known as "fireweed" due to its liking of sites cleared by fire, it is common and is often found on patches of cleared forestry.

Most usually but not always associated with rural areas, Sparrowhawks can be regular visitors to urban gardens too. This male often visited a garden in a Cork city suburb. After setting up a hide in the garden, I started my long wait. On the first day it flew through and then landed behind a tree so that I could just see its tail. It stayed there for a full twenty minutes before flying back to the nearby woodland without allowing me a picture. The next day it came quickly and caught a finch and immediately sped off into the distance. Finally, on my third day in residence it landed on top of the bird table and posed for this lovely portrait. ⇦

A Hedgehog climbs over a stump while looking for snails, worms and insects on a summer night. They hibernate during winter but are often out and about by February if the weather is mild.

The Wood Pigeon is found everywhere in Ireland and will come to gardens as well as fields and woodland. From a distance it is hard to see the subtle colours of its feathers, which are beautiful in close-up. ⇨

A Swallow's wings beat too fast for the camera to arrest their motion as it feeds its chicks without landing. These birds are majestic in flight and their arrival each year heralds the start of summer.

Both the male and female Mistle Thrush feed the chicks after they hatch. Here both adults are at the nest at the same time, with one having delivered food to the young as the other arrives with a bill full of tasty morsels. ⇨

The Blue tit is one of our most common birds but is no less beautiful because of this. In the intense light from the low sun on a winter's day, its delicate and colourful plumage is seen at its best. You need to be quick to get good pictures of these small birds as they visit the bird table, as even though they are usually unafraid of humans they move very quickly, not allowing much time for focusing and composition.

Essentially a butterfly of the woodland, the Silver-washed Fritillary can be found in open territory near to wooded areas also. These large and beautiful butterflies are easily recognisable and the under side of the wings have the unmistakable silver markings from which it take its name. This specimen has collected many marks and scratches on its wings during its lifetime.

The bright orange-yellow colour of the Jelly Antler Fungus makes it easy to find. The delicate stems grow from dead wood like gems adding some colour to the muted tones of the forest. ⇨

A Fallow deer buck rubs itself against a tree with the early morning mist giving it an almost ghostly appearance. Photographed in October during the annual rut, when the deer are at their most active, this buck was part of the herd of several hundred in Dublin's Phoenix park. The clash of antlers can be heard regularly at this time of year as the bucks spar for dominance.

House Sparrows are declining almost everywhere in Britain and Ireland but there are still a lot in places. Like most small birds they are very agile. This male would hang off the side of this stump at a garden feeding station and chase other birds away from the food.

*During a visit to a friend's orchard in September
I found Red Admiral butterflies feeding voraciously
on the fallen apples on the ground. A few like this
one were clinging to the apples still hanging from
the tree. These butterflies migrate to Ireland from
warmer southern areas during the summer months.*

The Robin with its bright red breast is probably the most recognised bird in our gardens. These little birds are very tolerant of humans and will follow gardeners around picking up grubs and worms. They have even been known to land on a person's hand to feed. They can however, be quite aggressive to other birds in the garden as the one in the main picture shows by ils stance. ⇦

Nature makes beautiful shapes and these Ferns are a great example. Like cartwheels on the forest floor, they will soon open up to resemble a shepherd's crook before turning into broad tapering fronds. ⇨

This Red Squirrel was a one of a few which were regular visitors to an urban garden in Cork city. They were attracted to the bird feeders full of peanuts and made visits at all times of the day from a small woodland which was just over the wall. I worked from a hide set up close to the feeders so the squirrels wouldn't be put off by my presence. On one occasion a squirrel arrived as I was positioning the hide but rather than turning to leave, it continued to feed proving that it was far more interested in the nuts than in me. ⇧

Strictly nocturnal, Long-eared Owls rest against tree trunks and in dense cover during the day but finding them is difficult. The "ears" which are actually just tufts of feathers, are held up to help blend into the background when at rest like this. Like all owls, they are truly beautiful and their soft downy feathers allow them to fly silently as they hunt for prey during the hours of darkness. ⇦

The grey/blue head of a male Chaffinch contrasts with the lovely orange/red of his breast as he enjoys the winter sunlight.

An Elephant Hawk moth rests on foliage on a garden wall during the day. Its incredible colours make this large moth easy to identify and beautiful to observe.

Having noticed the droppings on this metal gatepost I knew it was being used as a lookout post by a bird as it went to the nest. I set up and waited and before long this Dunnock arrived en-route to its young.

This Spotted Flycatcher and its mate had nested against this garden wall for three years in succession. They can be wonderful to watch as they sit on lookout posts and fly off suddenly to catch an insect in flight. You can often hear a sharp snap as they close their bill around the prey. Here the adult spreads its wings to fly from the nest having delivered food to the hungry chicks.

With the appearance of fine white china the Porcelain fungus is a delicate fungus usually associated with beech and oak trees. Bits of debris stick to its covering of slimy mucous as they fall from the trees above.

A Willow warbler tends to its chicks in the nest, which has been made close to the ground in a marshy area of woodland. These birds arrive to breed each summer in great numbers and can be found in a variety of habitats around the country.

A Starling uses its strong sharp claws to cling to the
rough wall outside its nest hole. From a distance
these birds look almost black but on closer inspection
you can see many spots and a variety of colours in
its feathers.

The shapes in nature sometimes
only become apparent when we
look at things closely. Self-heal
is an extremely common plant
which is regularly found in
garden lawns as well as in the
open countryside. The lovely
pastel colours and intricate shape
of this plant would go unnoticed
unless you get down to ground
level. ⇨

The vivid colours and striking design of the Peacock butterfly make it one of our most beautiful resident butterflies. This one was feeding on a white buddleia bush which is always a favourite for butterflies.

Greenfinches are one of our most common finch species. During winter they are often found in large groups and will sometimes descend on garden feeders in great numbers. This male is taking a break from feeding to enjoy the winter sunshine. ⇨

Not often seen, the Wood Mouse [also known as the Long-tailed Field Mouse] is common in Ireland. They are busy at night with a peak of activity around dusk and dawn, as they feed on seeds, fruits and insects. These mice live underground but often become prey to hunting owls as they scurry around wooded areas and ditches.

Inland
Waterways

As autumn takes hold, the colours in an Irish forest can be gorgeous, as seen in this riverside woodland. Beech trees in particular go through a spectacular metamorphosis as the seasons change.

The bright yellow pollen of a Willow catkin seems to glow in the spring sunlight. Butterflies, bees and moths will be attracted to this tree if they are on the wing during the early part of the year.

Although regarded as sea birds, many gull species, such as these squabbling Black-headed gulls regularly breed in colonies located on freshwater lakes. This pair were part of a large colony on an island on Lough Mask in Co. Mayo which was shared by Common gulls and some duck species also. ⇨

This Goldfinch was one of a flock of assorted finches that would come
to a seaside stream to bathe on a regular basis. I had positioned myself
close by to await their arrival and didn't bother using a hide. When the
birds arrived they were a little shy at first and perched in a nearby tree.
I remained still and after a while they realised that I was no threat and
one by one flew down and started to bathe.

While photographing the goldfinch opposite, I saw some Brown Rats scurrying around the fringes of the stream. One would regularly run into a drainage hole under a bridge nearby so I set myself up to make a picture as it came back out.

These common creatures are not everyone's favourite but they are very inventive and can be interesting to watch as they scurry about looking for food.

The Moorhen can be found on many of Ireland's waterways including many man made ponds and lakes where it becomes accustomed to the presence of man. In more isolated lakes it is often shy especially when nesting or rearing young and stays close to heavy vegetation where it can hide quickly.

A female Natterjack toad carries a male "in amplexus" for spawning. The smaller male climbs onto the back of the female and clasps her with his forelimbs and stays there until a suitable place for spawning has been found. In the springtime the males can be heard croaking loudly to the females to call them in to the spawning pools. These are the only toads in Ireland and are confined to a few small areas.

Spray and feathers fly as a Greylag Goose washes itself in the Lough in the heart of Cork city. Watching the activity on an urban lake like this can be wonderful, especially during the winter months when there are many species of ducks and gulls present also.

Water droplets run down the feathers of a Canada Goose as it stands on a platform in the early morning sunshine. This photograph was also taken at the Lough. Like the greylag goose it would not get a second look from serious bird watchers but birds like these are often the first contact children have with nature. It's a joy to watch youngsters being brought to feed the geese and ducks in a place like this and hopefully it will be the beginning of a life-long interest in nature. ⇦

Purple Loosestrife often grows in abundance on wet and marshy ground. Here they add their deep colour to the lakeside at Lady's Island in Co. Wexford.

While photographing various damselflies in close-up on a riverbank, I spotted this Beautiful Demoiselle male land on a nettle leaf nearby. Rather than try to get any closer I saw the opportunity for a wider shot, including the lovely dappled light on the foliage in the background. ⇨

This Fox moth caterpillar was climbing up a rush at the side of a small lake when I first saw it. As it got further up the stem it's weight bent the rush over until it was leaning against a water mint plant, which it duly climbed onto. ⇐

A male Pochard preens itself showing off the beautiful coppery red head and crimson eye that distinguish it so well. ⇧

This female Mallard actually had six chicks but the other four were
much slower than the two in the picture and seemed unable to keep up.
Here she stops and looks round as if to hurry the stragglers.

Sometimes called Kingcups, the bright
yellow, cup shaped flowers of the Marsh
Marigold livens up damp and marshy places
each spring. As the flowers age, the petals
flatten out showing a completely different
shape as shown in the second photograph.

The Large Red Damselfly is Ireland's only red damselfly and can be found all over the country. This one was photographed resting on a leaf close to a small ornamental garden pond.

A female Emerald Damselfly rests near the waters edge in the early morning sunlight. Also common and widespread, this one was photographed by a small bog lake in West Cork. ⇧

The drooping head of a Water Avens contrasts with the greens of the waterside woodland in the background. ⇨

Feathers, moss, leaves and sticks have been carefully packed around the eggs of a Mute Swan, to keep them warm while she takes a break from incubating to feed and wash in the river. ⇦

I watched this Four Spotted Chaser dragonfly as it flew around a small lake and noticed that it kept returning to this clump of grasses near the edge. To get in a suitable position to photograph it, I had to lie flat on the soggy borders of the lake and get very wet while waiting for it to return. These dragonflies are one of the most common in Ireland.

Common all around the country the Grey Wagtail is often found near water. This one with a bill stuffed full of flies shows their amazing ability to catch a large number of flies while in flight, keeping them all together until a sufficient number have been caught to feed their nestlings.

To photograph this Kingfisher bringing food to its chicks, I had to set up a hide in a very restricted space. It was so cramped that if I needed to stretch my legs, my feet would stick out from the hide. At one point a grey wagtail landed on the toe of my boot and sat there happily for about two or three minutes. ⇨

A female Banded Demoiselle damselfly holds its wings out to balance as it preys on another fly. These large damselflies have incredible shiny metallic bodies that almost look artificial.

Spray flies as a Dipper shakes the water from its wings having emerged from the river onto a favourite stone. These lovely little birds submerge themselves completely and walk along the bottom of fast flowing streams in search of tasty morsels.

This Blue-tailed Damselfly was resting on the ground enjoying the morning sunshine when I photographed it. It was very early and there were still some dewdrops on the mosses surrounding it.

The colourful Yellow Iris or Yellow Flag as it is sometimes known, grows abundantly on wet or marshy ground and can often cover large areas. The flowers themselves make wonderful shapes as the petals open up during the summer months.

Common Frogs can vary widely in colour, usually due to their particular habitat. I disturbed the one in the main picture as I walked in a boggy field. The peaty soil was almost black and the frog had become very dark also. After leaping out of my way, it became very still and allowed me to get down to ground level to make this front on portrait showing the high ridges of its eyes.

A walk in late summer near a pond or lake where frogs have spawned earlier in the year can reveal many tiny juvenile frogs feeding amongst the reeds and grasses. The one in the lower picture was only about one and a half centimetres long and almost gold in colour.

At a breeding colony in the west of Ireland, this Common Gull was fending off all the other gulls that tried to land on this rock. It would throw back its head and call loudly giving it the look of a baying wolf. ⇨

A Common Darter dragonfly rests on a stone in a garden rockery. This species is abundant in Ireland and can be seen from June through to October each year.

As autumn turns to winter, a visit to a waterfall on the upper reaches of a river can yield spectacular sights. Atlantic Salmon are now pushing their way up towards their spawning grounds. At this time of year the light levels are dropping and photographing this wonderful occurrence can be difficult with the fish travelling at tremendous speed. Timing is also crucial as there is no warning as to when the next one will appear from the water. Most of them have now changed from their silver beauty into the reds and browns of their spawning colours.

Farmland
and Moors

Photographing Badgers can be a frustrating business. Working most of the time in failing light or total darkness, a lot depends on whether the animals do as you hope they will do and go where you need them to go. I had been photographing them leaving the main entrance to this set when I realised there was another entrance under a fuchsia bush. The badgers seemed not to use it in general but I felt it would make a nice image with the red flowers showing.

After a few nights of feeding the animals at this entrance, they began to come to it but when they had fed they would go back in the way they had come and then exit from the main entrance.

By moving the feed a little further out of the entrance each night I finally coaxed them out a little further and got this image with the fuchsia bells overhead providing some nice colour.

A male Stonechat keeps watch for insects and possible predators on the highest part of a hedgerow. Every now and then he will fly down to the grass below to pick up a tasty morsel. If you venture too close, this little bird will scold you with its "tack-tack" call, which sounds like two pebbles being knocked together.

Marsh Fritillaries are one of our laziest butterflies. Unlike a lot of butterflies they are usually happy to remain still for long periods of time, especially on dull cooler days and allow a photographer to capture their beauty in their own time.

The Common Knapweed is an abundant plant in the countryside. Our usual viewpoint of a plant like this would be from above but by getting down to view it at its own level and looking at it in close-up, it is possible to see its beauty in a new way.

A walk in the Burren during spring can be a wonderful experience with thousands of Mountain Avens blooming across the landscape and growing from the roughest of ground. ⇦

The shell of the Common Field Grasshopper is like the armour of some alien being when looked at in close-up like this. It's quite difficult to get this close as they usually take fright when you approach. They use their powerful back legs to hop long distances in an attempt to disappear into the safety of long grasses.

Rabbits are common and widespread in Ireland and are often a pest to farmers. However I do like to watch them on a bright evening like this and see them all go on full alert with ears held high as I approach quietly. Any sudden movements or noises and they bolt for the cover of their burrows. ⇨

The bold colour, interesting shape and intricate patterns of Foxglove petals make a nice study. These plants often grow in such numbers that a whole ditch or hedgerow can appear to be coloured deep pink.

It is unusual to see a male Hen Harrier on the ground, especially during the breeding season when they hunt constantly for the female and chicks. I had been observing a pair with a friend and we noticed the male occasionally going to ground in a spot about one hundred metres from the nest site. When we investigated, we found a small clearing with a tree stump and a small area of low vegetation. I decided to place a well camouflaged remote control camera at the spot but couldn't be sure if the bird was landing on the stump or not. About four hours later the bird finally landed again and I fired two frames of film from some distance away. I had no idea what I had photographed. The results showed that the bird was landing to the side of the stump and not on it.

Because of this, only the bird's head is in sharp focus. I couldn't resist including these images in this book however, as this occurrence is not often recorded.

A Dog Violet pushes through the undergrowth in the springtime.
These small plants are abundant everywhere and decorate the
ditches with lovely dollops of colour early in the year.

The Brimstone butterfly flies early in the year and the midland counties are a great place to see them. When feeding or resting on a plant they always close their wings showing their unmistakable and interesting shape. On a warm May day there can be a lot of them on the wing but they can be incredibly flighty and difficult to photograph.

125

(previous spread) The Bank Vole, Ireland's only vole, is common in the south-west and appears to be spreading northwards slowly. These little mammals are experts at keeping hidden from human eyes as they move around in the undergrowth. Birds of prey are able to locate them more easily and they are regularly included in the diet of kestrels and owls.

Easily recognisable when seen from above with its wings open, the Orange Tip butterfly shows the very different and intricate detail on the underside of its wings when it holds them closed.

This Pied Wagtail had nested in a hole in this roadside wall. Each time it arrived back with food it would stop at the entrance to check for danger before going in.

I parked across the road and after a few minutes the bird became used to the presence of my car and continued to feed as I photographed it through the open window.

It is not always easy to find
groups of plants growing in such
a way as to make nice pictures.
Occasionally though you get
lucky, as I did when I came
across these five Common
Spotted Orchids growing in
such a perfect formation. ⇦

Barn Owls are creatures of habit and this bird was no exception.
Living in a busy farmyard barn it would regularly land with its prey
on the frame of a hen house, which was constructed against the barn,
and proceed to eat it. Here it has brought back an unfortunate bank
vole to banquet on.

An extremely common plant on ditches, walls and hedgerows, Herb Robert is easily overlooked. However, the little flower heads of this plant are particularly pretty when viewed closely. ⇧

Sand Martins are most usually photographed at their nest holes in sand and gravel banks and cliffs. This bird had excavated its hole in a place where there was a small shrub protruding from the cliff and often used it as a perch to rest on.

Pyramidal Orchids are striking plants and sometimes require a second look to truly appreciate the depth of colour in the petals. These two flowers were photographed on some waste ground where I found many species of orchid growing together. ⇨

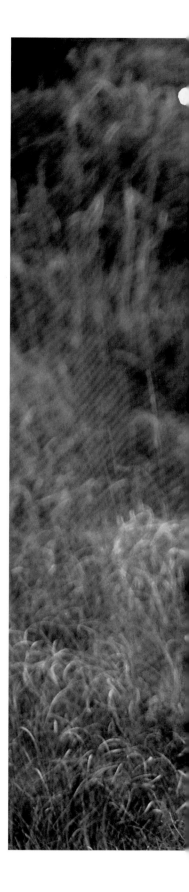

A female Wheatear scans her territory before taking her wriggling prey to waiting chicks. These birds are often some of the first of our summer migrants to arrive and may be seen from early March.

During the annual rut, which occurs in the autumn each year, the Red deer stags of Killarney National park bellow loudly across the mountains as they assemble their harem of hinds. Meeting a stag in full flight like this one can be a little unnerving but it is still a truly wonderful sight.

Four young Kestrel chicks look out of their purpose-built nesting box in a barn in Co. Tipperary. The farmer had noticed a pair of adults in the barn during one spring and erected a platform for them to use. These young were the third brood to be reared in successive years in this nest box. Having taken a few images of the adults arriving with food using a remote controlled camera, I couldn't resist making this close up image of the four chicks staring warily at me.

This male Kestrel would regularly rest at the entrance
to the nest hole where its mate was brooding her eggs.
The wall is part of a derelict church and the image was
shot using a well-camouflaged camera resting on an
adjacent wall and fired by remote control so as not to
upset the birds.

Frost clings to the bare flower stems of a Hogweed on a cold January morning.

Bog cotton is synonymous with Ireland and images of it appear on post cards and calendars on a regular basis. I came across this field full of it on a dull, breezy and damp day, but felt that this was probably a more typical scene on a moor than if the sun had been shining. ⇨

Ox-eye daisies are plentiful along ditches and roadsides during the summer and give a bright fresh feel to the landscape. With dark clouds filling the sky prior to a summer shower, I decided to photograph this group of plants from underneath, showing the white flower heads against the light. ⇧

The nocturnal Nightjar is an extremely rare summer visitor to Ireland with only a handful of breeding pairs arriving each year. The male birds call with a distinctive and strange "churring" from various vantage points in their territory as night falls. After extensive observation by two friends and myself, this stump was marked as a favourite calling spot for this male. The white markings on the tail feathers, which are seen clearly in this photograph, are absent in the female bird. ⇨

Another of the migrant butterflies to grace our land during the summer is the beautifully named Painted Lady. These elegant butterflies arrive from Africa from March or April and breed here during the summer months.

One of our most elusive mammals, the Irish Stoat is usually only seen for a fleeting moment as it searches out it's prey in a woodland or through the gaps in a stone wall. Often referred to as a weasel in error [we have no weasels in Ireland], they are not uncommon but due to their small size and their habits of searching for prey in heavy undergrowth and small crevices they often remain unnoticed. ⇦

The delicate petals of the Ragged-Robin look unkempt when viewed from a distance but their colour brightens up many a damp roadside and field in Ireland. There is also an old custom saying that it is unlucky to pick this pretty flower and bring it indoors.

The Bee Orchid is surely one of the most beautiful and interesting plants we have in Ireland and is always a delight to see. This plant was photographed in Co. Tipperary on a piece of waste ground where there was a mixture of orchids and an amazing ninety Bee orchids! The only day I was free to go to this site and photograph the plants was incredibly windy. With the help of the friend who had introduced me to the spot, I set up a windbreak using two coats suspended on sticks and my folding stool. This kept the flower steady so that I could make a sharp image. ⇨

A Sundew pushes up from the moss-covered ground of a moorland. This lovely little plant traps insects in its sticky "dew" and digests them to make up for the lack of nutrients in its chosen habitat. ⇦

This Sika deer doe and her fawn display the white rear ends that distinguish them from other Irish deer. This pair had been grazing at the side of a mountain road early one morning when I spotted them. As I approached quietly to photograph them, a car came down the mountain road at great speed as if the driver were late for work. The deer quickly ran onto the hillside and turned briefly to watch it pass before disappearing into the undergrowth.

Bees are always busy on warm days, moving from flower head to flower head in search of nectar. Usually they take no notice at all as you move close to watch them while they go about their business.

As young Foxes grow, they become more and more adventurous and inquisitive. I was photographing a group of cubs near the entrance to their den, when this one suddenly climbed a nearby wall and stayed motionless for a while as if on lookout duty for the rest of them. ⇨

Each morning, soon after it became light, this female Merlin would fly from her nest site to some rocks on an open moor. She would then preen, before calling for her mate to bring prey for the young chicks at the nest. On this occasion, it had been a wet misty night and preening took longer and was quite animated as she dried her feathers. To photograph this scene I had to be in my hide well before it got light. Being midsummer, I was in the hide by 3am but found that with the warm damp weather I had an uncomfortable wait, as it was occupied by about a million biting midges. These lovely falcons are Ireland's smallest bird of prey but are very rare with only a few pairs breeding in remote places each year. This pair successfully raised three chicks.

A Spring Gentian shoots from the
ground in the Burren in Co. Clare.
These dainty blue flowers are often
found in clusters and are one of the
most famous plants of the Burren
landscape. I chose to photograph this
single specimen because its petals
were so pristine. ⇦

The beautiful colour of the Common blue butterfly
always catches the eye as they flit across a meadow.
Here, a male and a female found copulating show
the underside of their wings with their intricate
patterns.

A Hoverfly feeds on a ragwort plant. These little flies, of which there are many species, are a joy to watch as they flit from plant to plant.

Many wild roses like this Dog Rose appear on our hedgerows during the summer months. They always brighten up the appearance of the wild ditches and if you find them nice and fresh like this one, you can see the perfection in nature's creations.

155

Three Peregrine falcon chicks, distinguished from the adult by their brown colouration, beg for food as an adult arrives with prey. The female had brooded her eggs behind the bush on the right. This made photography almost impossible until the chicks became large enough to roam around the ledge becoming more visible.

An Irish Hare grooms itself while being unaware of my presence. After taking a few pictures of this activity, I was hoping for a "classic" hare pose, with ears held up high and an alert look on its face. This one would not cooperate and by the time I had finished the batch of film in my pocket,

I had whistled at it, made barking noises and finally talked to it in an attempt to get the image I wanted. Eventually it stretched and sauntered away without allowing me the perfect pose but giving me many interesting images like this instead. ⇨

Wild Poppies add some beautiful colour to the landscape during the summer months. Here they have completely colonised a field of sugar beet. I had noticed the bright red field from quite a distance away as I was driving and followed the road around until I found what I felt was the best vantage point.

*Ireland's only reptile is the Common Lizard.
They hibernate during the winter months
emerging as the weather warms up in spring.
On hot days they enjoy basking on sand dunes
and walls like this one but can become prey to
kestrels hunting from above.*

*The Yellowhammer is a beautiful bird of the countryside but its
numbers are now in serious decline. Changing farming practices
with less grain being grown and more land used for grazing seems
to be one possible cause of this. Where they are still found it is
common to see two or three pairs in very close proximity to each
other, with the males, which are more brightly coloured than the
females, singing from the tops of bushes.* ⇐

A Corncrake calls on Tory Island off the coast of County Donegal. The strange cry of this bird was once familiar all over Ireland but is now limited to a few small areas of the country. The islanders work with wildlife and conservation groups to help keep disturbance during the breeding season to a minimum.

After two days hoping to photograph these elusive birds, I still had nothing to show and my last day on the island had arrived. At last one came out of the grasses and into clear view a short distance away from me and started calling. After taking a few frames and hoping the bird would move closer, the film in my camera finished.

As I reached for my waist bag, which contained many spare rolls, I realised with horror that I had left it in my hostel room. After all this time I felt totally foolish. The bird duly disappeared. I went back to collect my film and feeling very despondent I went out again in search of a picture.

With about 20 minutes to go before I was due to take the ferry back to the mainland and ready to admit defeat, this bird suddenly jumped up on top of a garden wall close by. My perseverance had paid off. This lovely image, of a bird close to extinction but still calling out proudly, will stay with me always.

Notes on the photography

When I decided to produce this book I knew it might take a while and prove difficult, if not impossible, to do everything that I wanted to. Both were true. However, for every disappointment I had there was something positive just around the corner. For some of the subjects I photographed I had preconceived ideas about the result I wanted to achieve, but, inevitably, the final image turned out to be a little, if not totally, different. Wildlife does as it wants and this is how it should be. There were occasions when I could only sit and watch as something amazing unfolded before my eyes but the light was not good enough to photograph the event. At other times I was lucky that everything came together and situations or the behaviour of the subject actually improved on my initial hopes. Most of all I had a lot of fun creating these images, even when sitting in a cramped hide on the coldest of days.

Nature photography is often as much about good planning as it is about the ability to see and make beautiful pictures. You need to be in the right place at the right time and be prepared for the action. Many hours are often needed to prepare and place a hide in just the right position.

Days or weeks are sometimes spent just observing your subject and its behaviour before starting the photography. When you do begin to make your pictures, you need to know that the equipment you have chosen will do the job it was designed for with the minimum of fuss. While the technology should not take over from the art of photography, a photographer needs to be truly confident that the camera will perform reliably to get the best possible results.

While all professional photographers seem to amass vast amounts of equipment over their working life, nature photographers seem to collect even more than the rest. Moving from photographing birds in flight, to fungi on a forest floor and then to badgers leaving their sett as the light fades, requires a range of equipment which differs as much as the subjects themselves. Because of this, the nature photographer must work with a camera system that is built to deal with all these different situations as they arise. For those interested in the technical side of my photography, here are some points that may be of interest.

CAMERAS AND LENSES.

All the pictures in this book were made using the Canon EOS equipment. Two EOS 1n camera bodies provided the backbone for my system. These cameras get a lot of hard knocks when I'm out and about and they cope with this very well. During the two to three years that it took me to complete this project, they have never missed a beat despite being rained upon, dragged up marshy mountains, used on windswept sandy beaches and being dropped on more than one occasion. While I do try to take care of my cameras, accidents do happen, and these cameras were able to deal with all the trials I threw at them.

The lenses I use range from a 17-35mm F2.8 zoom, up to the 600mm F4 super telephoto. For close up and macro work I use both the 50mm F2.5 and a 180mm F3.5 micro lenses.

Extension tubes of 14mm and 25mm and 1.4x and 2x tele-extenders are also vital to the work I do. The quality of these lenses and accessories is just superb. When photographing birds and animals I try to show the beautiful detail and texture in the subjects and these lenses do this nicely.

When giving slide show and lectures I am often asked about the advantages of autofocus over manual focus. I will admit that I was slow to believe that the autofocus revolution that swept across the world of cameras would really benefit photographers. The early models were slow and not very accurate. However once I had tried the EOS camera and lens system, my mind was changed forever. The system is smooth, silent and ultra fast, which is of utmost importance when photographing moving subjects like birds. Most of the lenses in this system also offer you the advantage of being able to revert to manual focus without even flicking a switch, so the die-hard manual photographers are not left out.

For flash lighting I use two Canon 540EZ flash units. These are used both on camera and off camera using dedicated connecting cords. This system is used for many different situations and gives uniformly excellent results. Badgers leaving a sett or Pine Martens foraging over the rocky terrain of the Burren in Co. Clare are both dealt with superbly. The system can be used as the main light source or as a supplementary light for fill in with equal ease.

FILM.

Most photographers have a favourite film type and I am no different in this respect. For the most part, the pictures in this book were made using Fuji Sensia II, 100asa slide film. A few were shot on Fuji Provia or Fuji Velvia. Sensia II combines excellent detail, fine grain structure and accurate colour rendition with a medium speed. This makes it a perfect choice for the sometimes less than perfect light conditions we have to work with here in Ireland. It is important for a photographer to get to know a film well if he or she is to get the best from it. Having tried and tested a number of films over the years I am happy to use Sensia II as my film stock for almost all my work. During the completion of this project I have exposed thousands of frames in many different lighting conditions. Whether photographing Red deer stags on the cloud covered mountains of Killarney National

park in October, or Puffins on the Saltee islands in strong early morning sunlight in June, this film never let me down. Its consistency is superb and this gives me the confidence to know that the results are going to be what I expect. At night, with the necessity to use artificial flash as the only light source, Sensia II still performs with the excellence I require, keeping detail in both the highlights and the shadow areas of the final image. Some of the images in this book were made when light levels required a higher film speed. In most cases I still used Sensia but "pushed" it to a higher rating and changed the processing accordingly. A trained eye might notice the images that were made in this way but the results are still excellent. Fuji are constantly upgrading their film. Since I started this project they have released 100asa Provia F [fine grain] and up dated their 400asa Provia also. From reports I've heard these films are both magnificent and I will be trying them as soon as possible.

ACCESSORIES

Apart from the cameras and accessories mentioned above, a few pieces of equipment have proven themselves invaluable to me over the years. Camera shake is the greatest enemy of sharpness in a photograph and a good tripod is essential for keeping cameras and lenses steady. I have two main tripods for everyday use. The versatile Benbo Pro Mark 2 is fantastic for photographing plants, flowers and insects as it can twist itself into all sorts of positions. My other tripod is the super strong Gitzo 410 which is immensely sturdy and robust.

For the work I do which doesn't require my biggest lenses, a ball and socket tripod head is used. However when using the 600mm lens which weighs in at more than 14lbs. I find that I need something that provides more rigidity whilst still giving plenty of manoeuvrability. For this I use a Wimberley tripod head. The Wimberley is one of the most useful and innovative photography accessories I have come across. Designed in the USA it is designed on the same principle as a ships compass, which is always self-righting. When set up correctly, a lens of any size or weight can be balanced perfectly, making it feel almost weightless. At the same time it can be instantly moved to focus on a moving subject. I simply wouldn't be without it.

FIELD WORK

The most important thing in wildlife photography is to know your subject and its behaviour. Apart from a great deal of time spent photographing each subject, I often spend hours and sometimes even days observing my quarry without a camera. In this way I can get to know a subject intimately. There are inevitably some missed photographic opportunities but the extra insight gained into the lifestyle of an animal is invaluable when the photography does start. Wild animals are often creatures of habit, following a similar pattern of behaviour each day and a good knowledge of this is often the key to making a good image.

Forward planning is also of utmost importance. The seasons come and go with surprising rapidity and wildlife moves with them. Being prepared to get up and go when things are at their best is imperative. Birds rear their young extremely quickly, for instance, and once the young can fly and fend for themselves they are no longer rooted to one spot, making them harder to pin down for a picture. The same is true of mammals. When plants bloom there is usually only a day or two in which to catch them at their best after which the petals start discolouring or become disfigured due to the attention of insects. Keeping an eye on all these things is vital when photographing the natural world. While I try to get this insight with many of my subjects, time is often a restricting factor and when this is the case I must rely on the knowledge of others. There are many people who helped me during the time I worked on this book and I hope I have remembered them all on the "Acknowledgements" page at the start of the book. Without their knowledge and observations some of these images simply wouldn't have been made.

Most animals are aware of their surroundings and changing their habitat by erecting a hide to photograph from or changing the landscape in any way can distress them if care isn't taken. The guiding principle should always be that no picture is worth an animal's distress or even worse an adult abandoning its young. When introducing a hide or some camera equipment into the vicinity of an animal especially one with young I try to do it in stages. This can often take days but is worth it if there is no disruption to the natural rhythm of things. While I do have a prefabricated hide, I prefer where possible to create a place to work from using the natural surroundings. Bushes and ditches can often be modified with a little effort to accommodate a person with a camera and this can work to great effect and give much better cover than a purchased hide. I have even had a group of hikers pass within a few feet of me when in such a position without having the slightest idea of my presence.

Because of my love of nature I am passionate about keeping the landscape clean and I hate seeing litter dumped in our wild places. It is all too common that I hop over a ditch to see what I can find only to be confronted with three of four black plastic refuse sacks which have been thrown from a car by someone

who doesn't care for our wonderful countryside. It was with a certain sense of irony, that when photographing one of the more illusive subjects in this book I chose to use an abandoned car as a hide! I had been checking out the habitat in question and realised that my subject regularly used a set of rocks in quite open countryside as look out positions. A normal hide would stand out like a sore thumb so another option was needed. Close to these rocks three old cars had been dumped to rot. My first reaction was disgust that someone could dump old cars to disintegrate slowly in the Irish countryside. I soon realised however that the 1970's Ford Cortina was actually in a fantastic position from which to observe the rocks without being noticed. The bird in question was accustomed to these cars and so by blocking the windows with some scrim netting I was able to use it as a ready made hide. I even had a more comfortable seat than usual, as some of the foam seat padding [which of course is not biodegradable] was still present. There was definitely a sense that I was colluding with those who deface the environment but I think most people are learning that we must stop these practices now before the whole country becomes a rubbish tip.

AND FINALLY

All in all I had a great deal of fun working on this project. We have an abundance of natural beauty in Ireland and we should be proud and thankful for this. I hope you have enjoyed the pictures in this book and that they encourage you to view and photograph our wildlife with renewed interest.

Mike

Further reading on Ireland's wildlife

Exploring Irish Mammals
By Tom Hayden and Rory Harrington.
TownHouse. ISBN: 1860590934.

Complete Guide to Ireland's Birds - Second Edition
by Eric Dempsey and Michael O'Clery,
Gill & MacMillan, 2002. ISBN: 0-7171-3401-6.

Ireland's Marine Life. A World of Beauty.
Editors Matt & Susan Murphy. Photography: Paul Kay et al.
Sherkin Island Marine Station. ISBN: 1-870492-75-7.

Ireland's Bird Life. A World of Beauty.
Editors Matt & Susan Murphy. Photography: Richard Mills.
Sherkin Island Marine Station. ISBN: 1-870492-80-3.

A Beginner's Guide to Ireland's Seashore
Helena Challinor, Susan Murphy Wickens, Jane Clark, Audrey Murphy
Photography: Paul Kay and Terry Farnell.
Sherkin Island Marine Station. ISBN: 1-87-049296-X.

The Wild Plants of Sherkin, Cape Clear and Adjacent Islands of West Cork
by John Akeroyd (editor), Lucy Wright, Jennifer Shockley, Karen Clarke, Nick Rowe, Pat Hatch,
Mike Robinson, Beth Milner.
Sherkin Island Marine Station. ISBN: 1-870492-86-2.

Nature in Ireland - A Scientific and Cultural History
Edited by John Wilson Foster and Helena C.G. Chesney
Lilliput Press, Dublin 1997 ISBN: 1-874675-295.

Flora Hibernica – The Wild Flowers, Plants and Trees of Ireland.
by Jon Pilcher and Valerie Hall.
Collins Press. ISBN: 1-903464-03-X.

Kerry – A Natural History.
by Terry Carruthers.
Collins Press. ISBN: 1-898256-45-4.

Wild Plants of the Burren and Aran Islands
by Charles E. Nelson.
Collins Press. ISBN: 1-898256-70-5.

A Place to Treasure: Killarney National Park.
Edited by Bill Quirke.
Collins Press. ISBN: 1-898256-69-1.

The Way That I Went. An Irishman in Ireland.
New Introduction by Michael Viney. By Robert Lloyd Praeger.
Collins Press. ISBN: 1-898256-35-7.